- This is for my amazingly strong girl. We have been through a long journey but know Mama and Daddy will always be by your side. You make us so proud! We love you Princess. Keep reaching for the stars!

Love Mama

- I'd like to say a huge thank you to my Mom and Dad (Brenda & Carl). You guys have been our rock through everything and never left our side. We are incredibly lucky to have you both to lean on. We love you so much!

Hi, my name is Claire and I have external fixation devices on both legs, but I like to call them frames.

The frames were placed on my legs during a surgical procedure. I needed the frames to help get my legs to be straight.

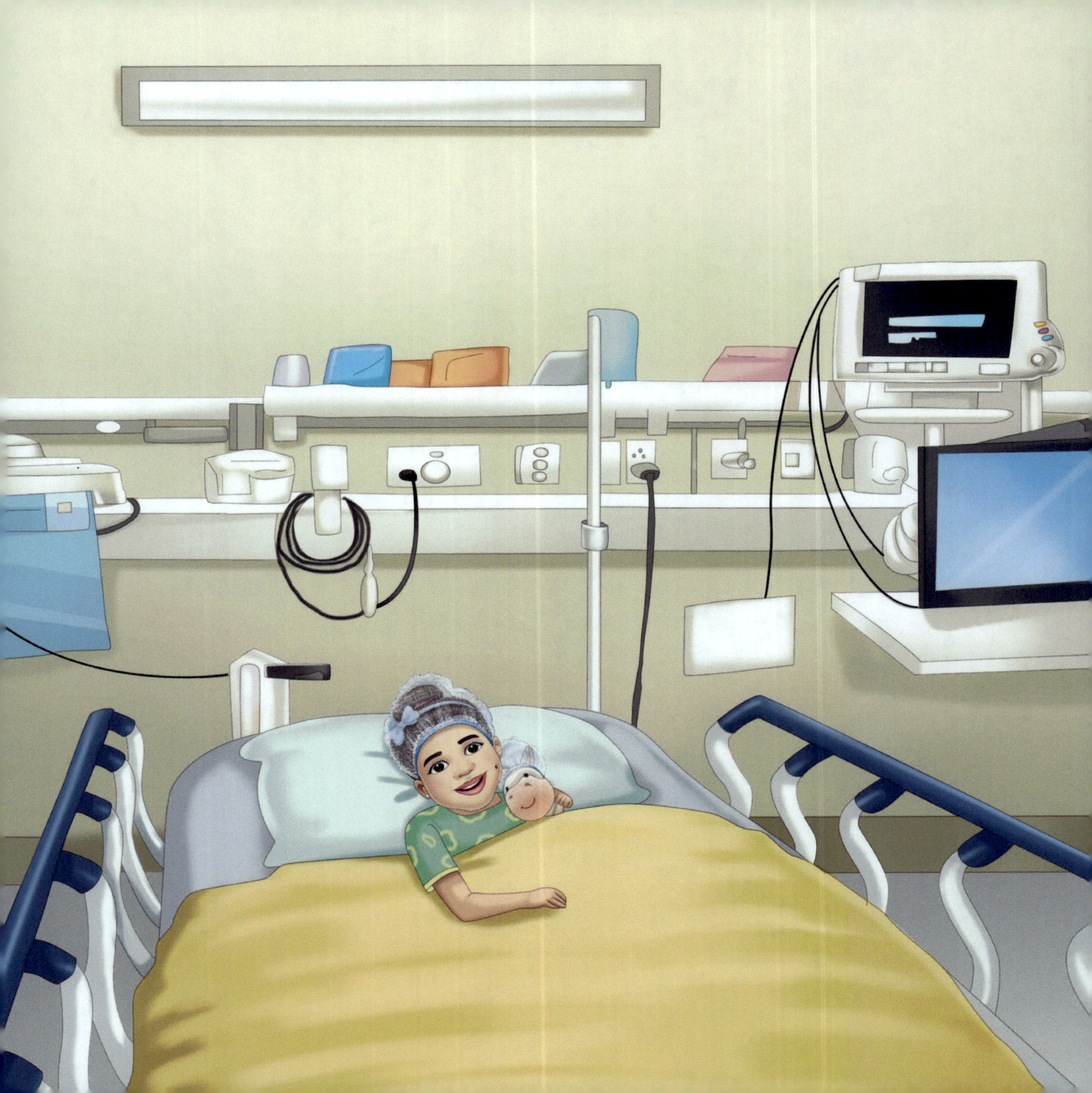

I was born with skeletal dysplasia, that's a big word meaning my bones grow a little differently

My legs were bent, and I had trouble walking and they would sometimes give me pain.

The best way to help me was getting frames.

My surgery day came quickly, and I was ready!
We arrived at the hospital.

HOSPITAL

Mama and daddy got to stay with me and Nana and Papa waited for me in the waiting room.

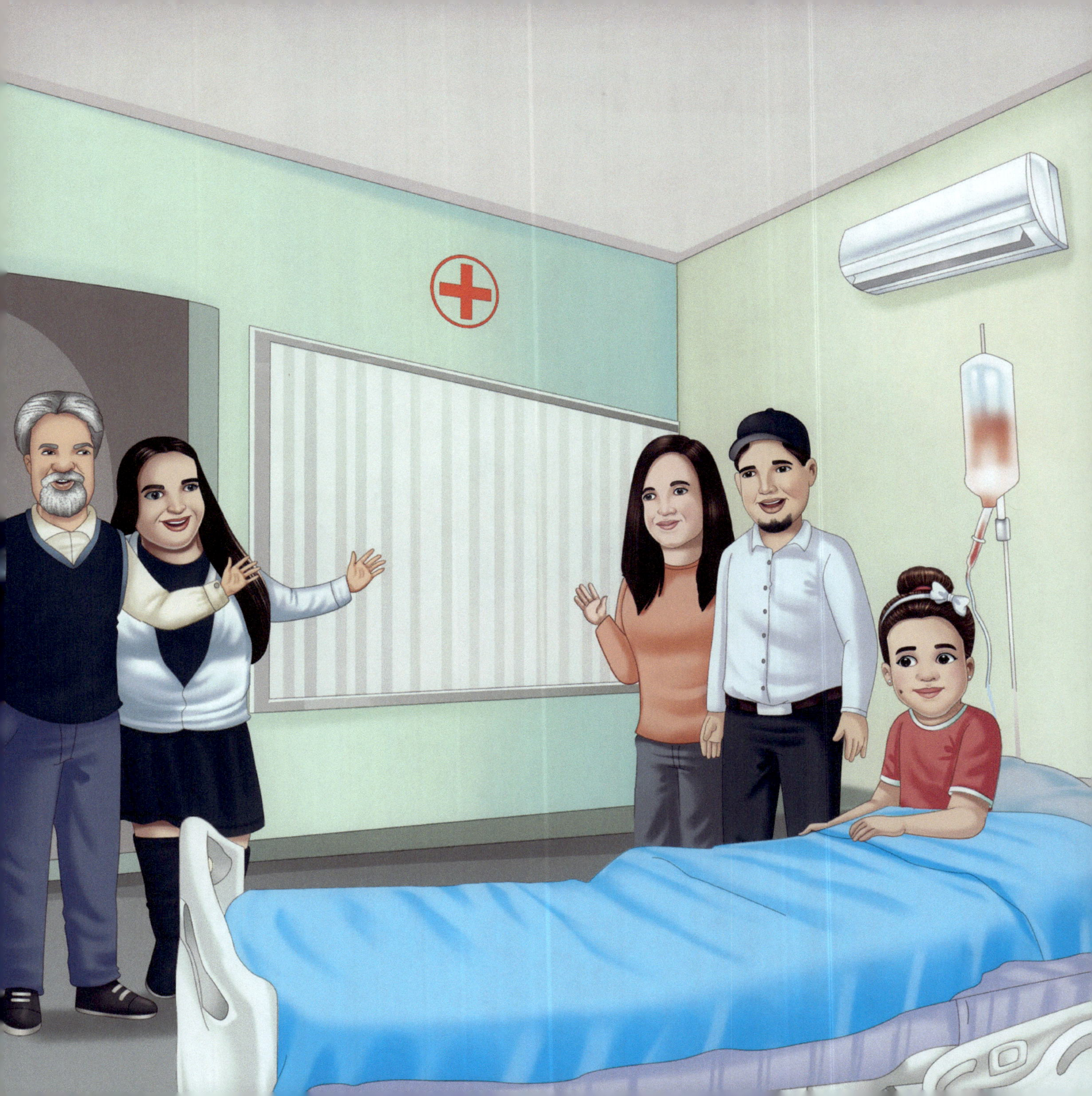

I got to drink a special cherry drink that made me sleepy.
I fell asleep.

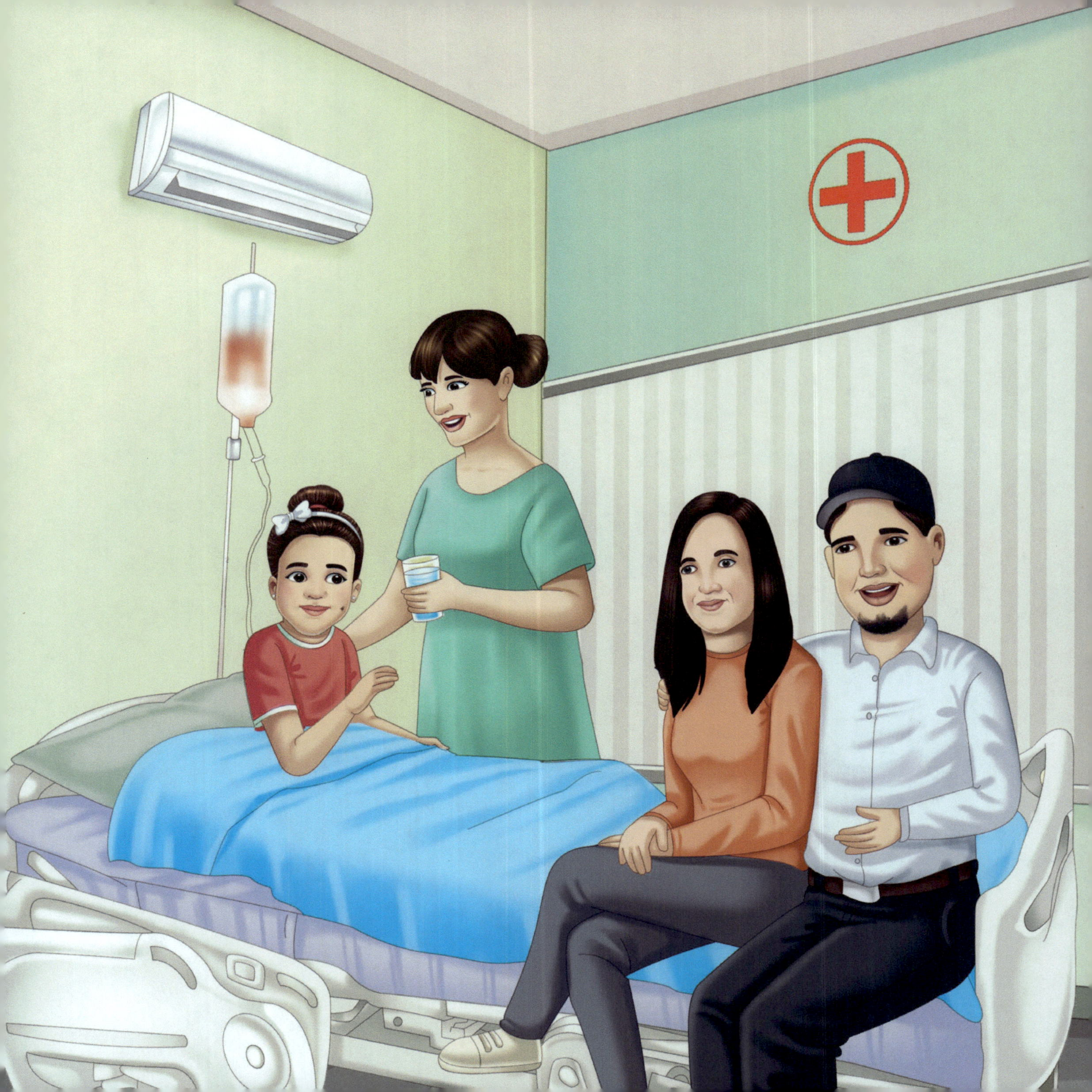

When I woke up, I was in the recovery room with Mama and Daddy next to me. I didn't even know my surgery was all done. I went up to my hospital room that I had to stay in for three days just to make sure everything was ok.

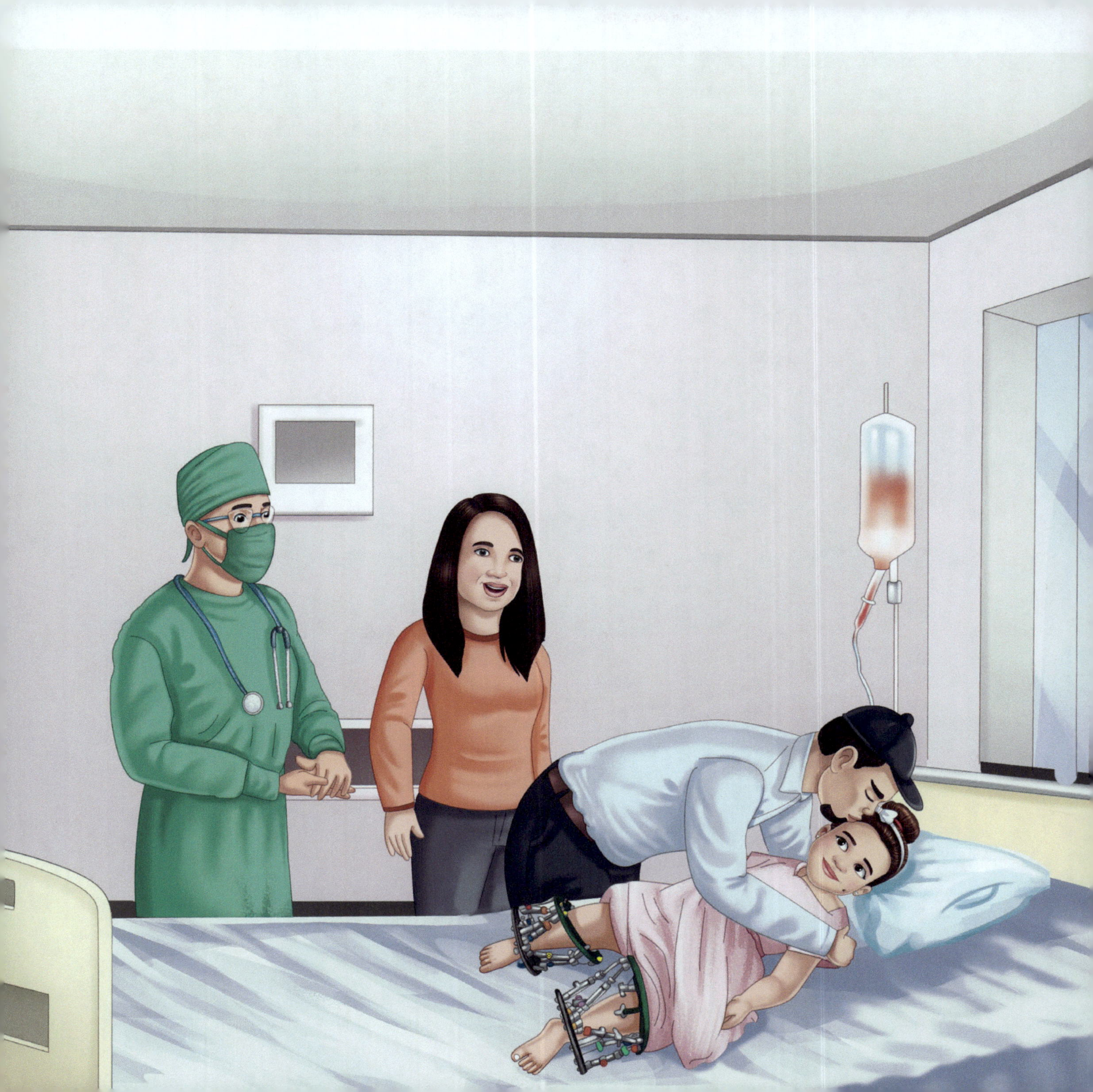

Those three days went by slowly, but Mama got to stay with me the whole time and my family got to visit me too!

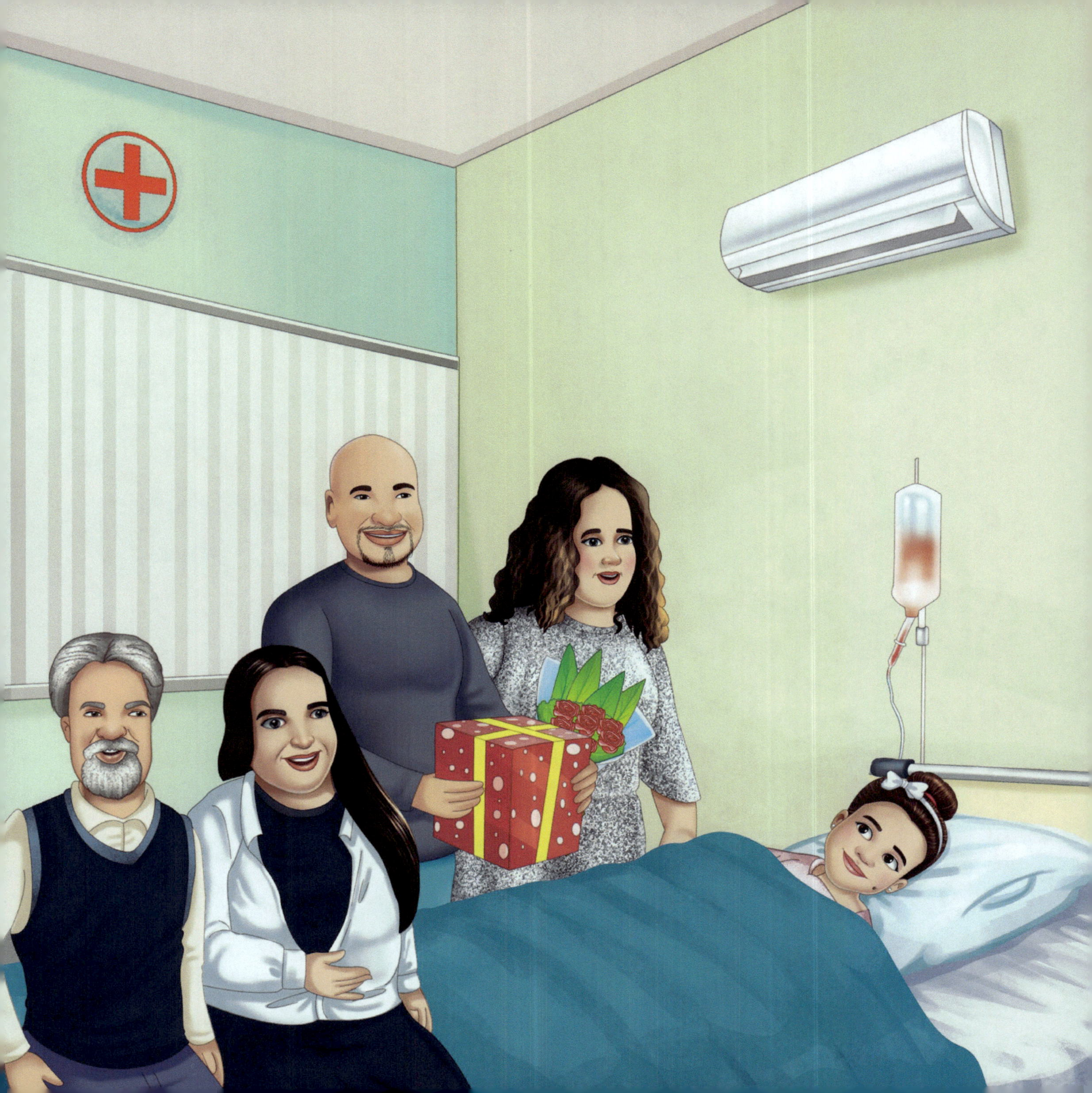

When we came home it was a little scary, my frames were heavy and hard to move. They had special numbers and colors.

The numbers helped Mama, because every day we had to move my legs to a certain number until my legs were completely straight. It didn't hurt to move them because we went slowly, it just felt tight.

Once my legs were straight, we no longer had to ajust them, and I was able to begin my healing.

Healing took some time, but I was able to get up and walk again with the help of a walker.

I was doing well!

But then I got an infection in both legs. I got medicine but unfortunately that didn't help, and my doctor thought it would be best to take my frames off early.

I went to the hospital and got my sleepy cherry drink and off to surgery to remove my frames.

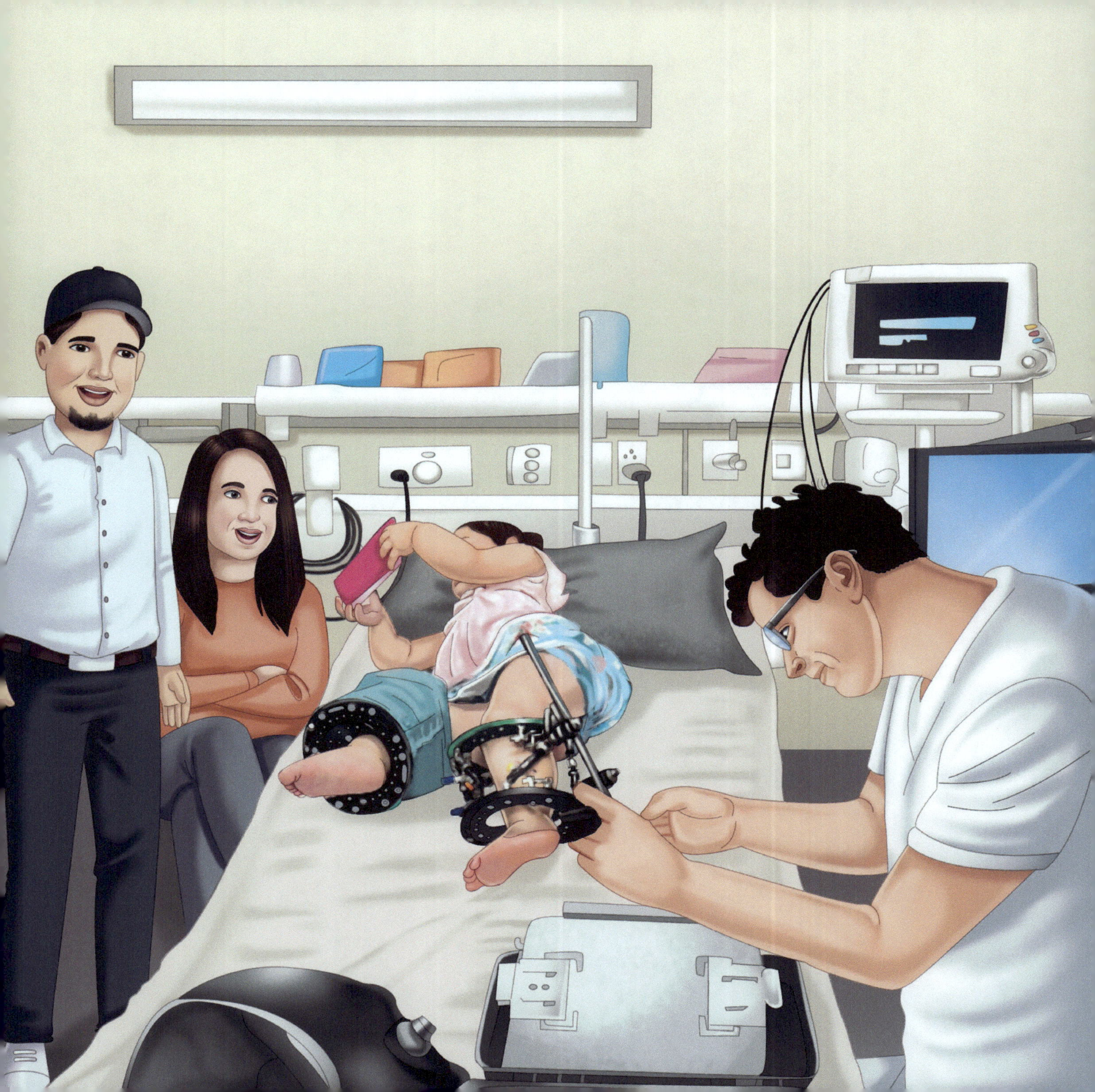

My doctor said since my frames had to be taken off early, I would need to get casts for the rest of my healing time.

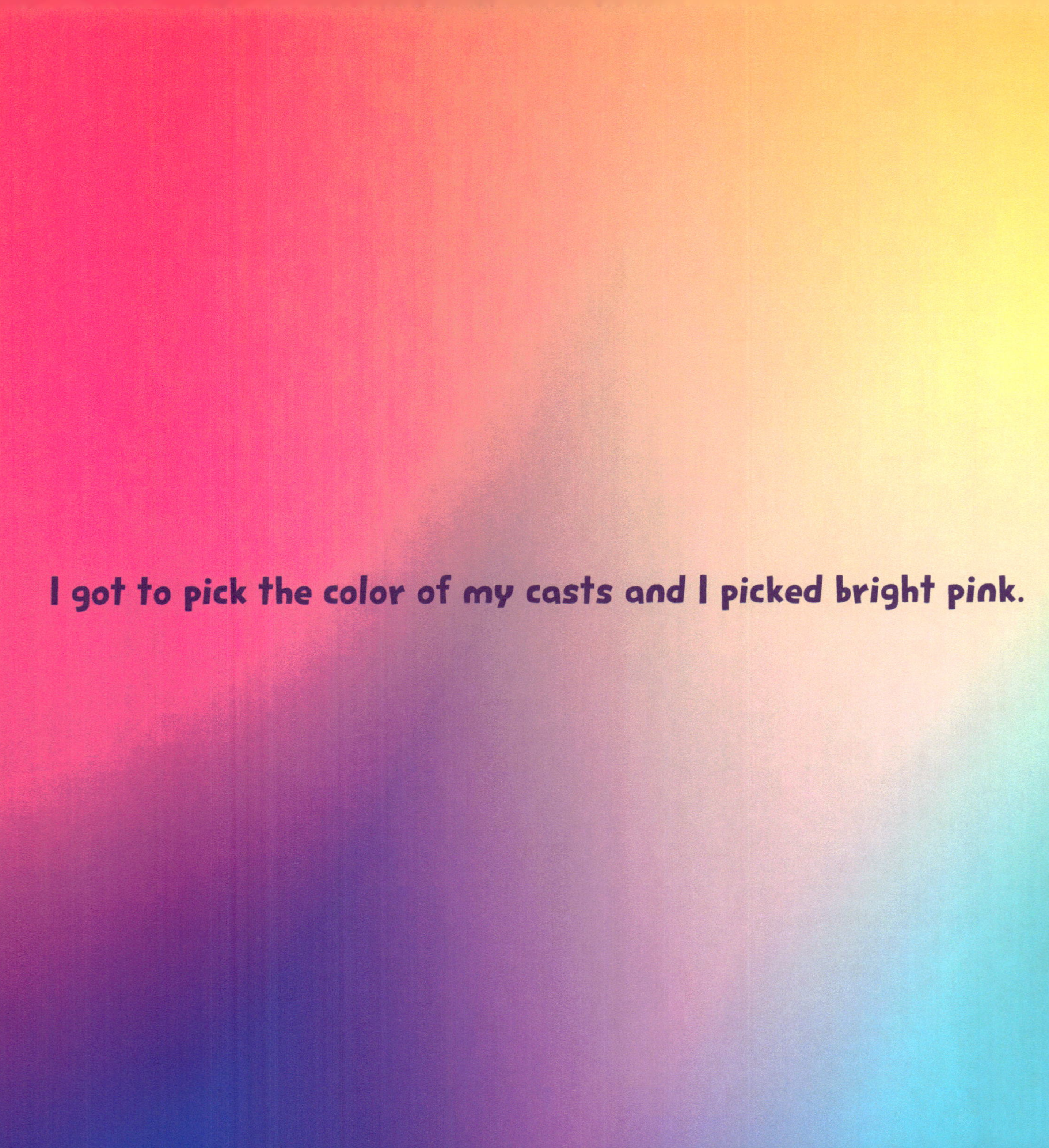
I got to pick the color of my casts and I picked bright pink.

The surgery didn't take very long, as soon as I woke up and drank some juice, I was able to go home. I didn't even have to stay overnight.

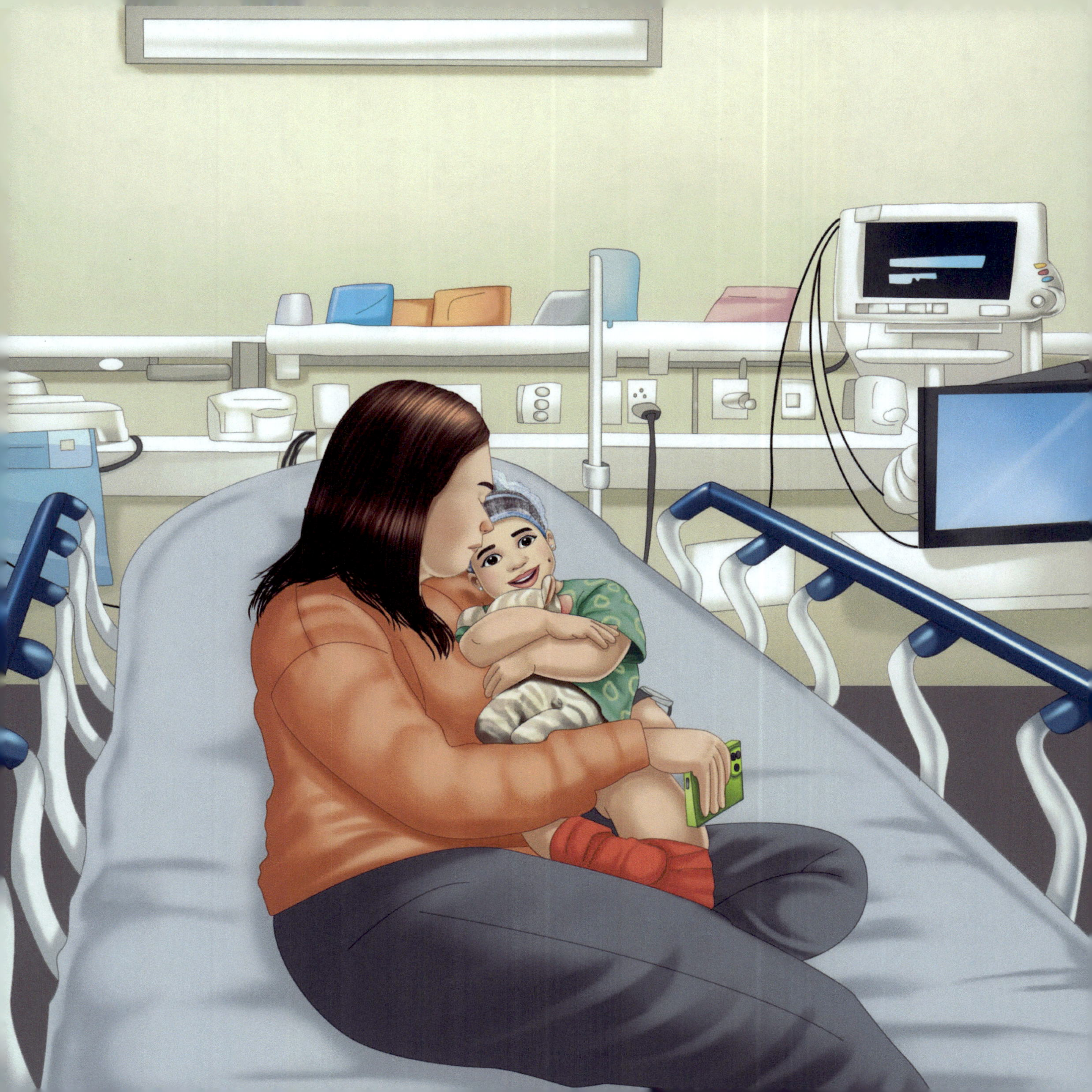

My casts had to stay on for a little while.

After wearing casts a bit I got braces that I could take on and off my legs.

The whole process took a long time but I'm happy I got it done.
I don't have to worry about leg pains.

Crooked legs held me back but no more.
Thanks to my frames!